ACKNOWLEDGEMENTS

These quotations were gathered lovingly but unscientifically over several years and/or
were contributed by many friends or acquaintances. Some arrived—and survived
in our files—on scraps of paper and may therefore be imperfectly worded or attributed.
To the authors, contributors and original sources, our thanks, and where appropriate,
our apologies. –The Editors

CREDITS

Written by Dan Zadra and Kobi Yamada
Designed by Sarah Forster

ISBN: 978-1-932319-86-6

2nd Printing. 06 10   Printed with soy ink in China

WHAT ARE LITTLE BOYS MADE OF?

WRITTEN BY *Dan Zadra and Kobi Yamada*
DESIGNED BY *Sarah Forster*

COMPENDIUM™
INCORPORATED

**EVERY GREAT MAN
WAS FIRST A BOY.**

~Dan Zadra

WHAT ARE LITTLE BOYS MADE OF?

SNAKES & SNAILS
& CRAZY TALL TALES...

and
HOPES & DREAMS...

A<small>ND</small>
S<small>TRENGTH</small>

&

C<small>OURAGE</small>...

& IMAGINATION & DARING...

and GIFTS & TALENTS...

&YEARNING

&LEARNING...

and FAITH

& OPTIMISM...

AND
PURPOSE

and
MEANING...

& WARMTH
and TENDERNESS...

& ADVENTURE

& ENTHUSIASM...

& CARING

 UNDERSTANDING...

& HONOR
& INTEGRITY...

AND
FAMILY

and
FRIENDSHIP...

&

LOVE

and LOYALTY...

AND JOY

and LAUGHTER...

& MOMENTS
& memories...

FOX.

& SUCCESS

and

SATISFACTION...

...& ALL THINGS POSSIBLE.

THAT'S WHAT LITTLE
BOYS ARE MADE OF.